The True Story of

POCAHONTAS

Colleen Adams

PowerKiDS press

New York

Published in 2009 by The Rosen Publishing Group, Inc.
29 East 21st Street, New York, NY 10010

First Edition

Editor: Nicole Pristash
Book Design: Kate Laczynski
Photo Researcher: Jessica Gerweck

Photo Credits: Cover, pp. 5–15 © Getty Images, Inc.; p. 17 © Superstock.com; pp. 19, 21 © North Wind/North Wind Picture Archives.

Library of Congress Cataloging-in-Publication Data

Adams, Colleen.
    The true story of Pocahontas / Colleen Adams.
        p. cm. — (What really happened?)
    Includes index.
    ISBN 978-1-4042-4475-7 (library binding)
    1. Pocahontas, d. 1617—Juvenile literature. 2. Powhatan women—Biography—Juvenile literature. 3. Smith, John, 1580–1631—Juvenile literature. 4. Rolfe, John, 1585–1622—Juvenile literature. I. Title.
    E99.P85P571433 2009
    975'.01092—dc22

                                                    2007051954

Manufactured in the United States of America

CONTENTS

WHO WAS POCAHONTAS?

Pocahontas was a Native American woman who lived with her **tribe**, the Powhatan, in Virginia, in the early 1600s. She made friends with the first English **colonists**, who came to settle the **colony** of Jamestown, Virginia. She helped the colonists learn how to farm and live life in their new home.

There are many different stories about Pocahontas's life and her friendship with John Smith, a leader of the colony. Many believe some of these stories are not true. Do you want to know what really happened? Let's take a look at the story of one of history's most interesting women.

Pocahontas's life story is very famous. Many books and movies have been made about it. However, some of the stories told about Pocahontas's life might be untrue.

THE PLAYFUL ONE

Pocahontas was born in 1595 in the part of Virginia known as the Tidewater. Her father, Chief Powhatan, was the leader of the Powhatan tribe. Pocahontas's mother was sent away shortly after she gave birth to Pocahontas. Chief Powhatan had many wives. It was Chief Powhatan's **custom** to send away his wives after they gave birth.

Pocahontas's real name was Matoaka. When she was little, Pocahontas liked to run, jump, and have fun. She loved to play and would often cause a stir in her village. The Powhatans decided to call her Pocahontas, which means "playful one."

Chief Powhatan (right) was very powerful. English colonists would offer gifts to Powhatan in return for his friendship and the friendship of his tribe.

THE NEW COLONY

In December 1606, some people in England decided to sail across the ocean to start a new life in a new land. They dreamed of the riches they would make there. After many months, they reached the coast of Virginia on May 14, 1607. They called their settlement Jamestown.

Life was hard at first. Many colonists did not know how to grow their own crops. The colonists also found that the Powhatan tribe already lived there. The Powhatans and the colonists got along with each other at first, but soon the colonists started taking more land. This made the Powhatans angry.

Here the colonists and the Powhatans are seen trading goods with one another. The colonists gave the Powhatans tools and guns, and the Powhatans gave the colonists food.

9

CAPTURE OR CUSTOM?

That winter, some of the colonists and their leader, John Smith, **explored** the land. Smith ended up on the Powhatans' land, and they **captured** him. Smith later said that the Powhatans placed his head on a stone. They stood over him with clubs, waiting for their chief's orders. Pocahontas begged her father to free Smith. Chief Powhatan let him go only because Pocahontas had asked.

Some **historians** do not believe Smith's story. They think what happened was a Powhatan **ritual** and the Powhatans did not plan to hurt him. Little is known about the Powhatan tribe, so we may never know the truth.

In 1624, Smith wrote a book, called The Generall Historie of Virginia, New England, and the Summer Isles. *In it, he describes his capture by the Powhatans. Many think that Smith made up parts of the story.*

This picture shows Pocahontas saving John Smith. However, some think the Powhatans were only doing a ritual, in which they took Smith in as part of their tribe.

11

GOOD FRIENDS

After Smith was freed, Pocahontas began visiting Jamestown. She was 11 years old then. Pocahontas brought food to the colonists and played games with the children. Her help saved many colonists from **starvation**. While visiting, Pocahontas and John Smith became good friends. Smith taught Pocahontas some English words, and she taught Smith how to say things in her language.

Some stories say that Pocahontas and John Smith were in love. It is now believed, however, that they were just friends. Pocahontas was too young for Smith. Pocahontas just wanted to help Smith and the other colonists understand her tribe.

Here John Smith is seen giving a small gift to Pocahontas. Many people believe John Smith and Pocahontas were like brother and sister, and they were not in love.

13

SMITH LEAVES JAMESTOWN

Three years later, in 1610, several ships from England brought hundreds of new colonists to Jamestown. Many of them did not treat the Powhatans well. Smith often had to settle fights between the colonists and the Powhatans. Because of this, some colonists wanted a new leader.

John Smith later returned to America in 1614, but he never went back to Virginia. He visited the coasts of Maine and Massachusetts. Smith named this place New England.

Later that year, Smith was badly hurt in an **explosion**. He decided to go back to England to live. Smith sailed away and never returned to Jamestown. He never got the chance to say good-bye to Pocahontas so the colonists told Pocahontas that Smith had died.

This picture shows new ships arriving in Jamestown in 1610. The new colonists brought much-needed food and supplies to the struggling settlement.

15

TAKEN AWAY

A few years later, Pocahontas's life changed completely. When she was 18, Pocahontas was **kidnapped** by some of the English colonists, led by Captain Samuel Argall. Argall told Chief Powhatan he would trade Pocahontas for the English colonists Powhatan had captured earlier. Argall also wanted the guns and corn Powhatan had stolen from the colonists. Powhatan let the captured colonists go but did not give Argall the other things he wanted. The colonists kept Pocahontas.

At first, Pocahontas was afraid, but the colonists treated her well. The colonists became her friends, and they taught her the English language.

Some people think Chief Powhatan did not try to get Pocahontas (middle) back after her kidnapping, shown here. He thought Pocahontas could help the two groups get along again.

17

A NEW WAY OF LIFE

The colonists kept Pocahontas with them for over a year while they waited for Powhatan to give them what they wanted. After a while, though, Pocahontas became used to living like the English settlers. She had given up her Native American language and **lifestyle**.

When Pocahontas was set free, she decided to stay with the settlers. She married a colonist, named John Rolfe, when she was 19 and took the name Lady Rebecca Rolfe. Some people think Pocahontas was forced to marry Rolfe. Others think it was likely that she was happy with her new family. What is the true story?

On January 30, 1615, Pocahontas and John Rolfe had a son, shown here. They named him Thomas.

A GREAT HONOR

In 1616, Pocahontas and her family traveled to London, England. There, Pocahontas met King James I and Queen Anne of England. The king and queen wanted to show the English that Native Americans were not bad people.

When John Smith heard that Pocahontas was coming to London, he wrote a letter to Queen Anne. He told her about all the ways that Pocahontas had helped the English colonists.

Many parties were given to honor Pocahontas for the ways she helped the English settlers. They treated her with kindness and respect. Pocahontas also found out that John Smith was alive. They spoke to each other, but their friendship never continued. Sadly, during the trip back to Virginia, Pocahontas became very sick on the ship and died. She was only 22 years old.

21

WHAT REALLY HAPPENED?

There are only a few written records of Pocahontas's life. One of them is a letter that John Smith wrote. Many believe he made up some of what he wrote in that letter so it is hard to know the truth. Did Pocahontas save John Smith? Did she and Smith fall in love? Was Pocahontas forced to live a life she did not want to live? Some of these questions may never be answered.

Despite the mysteries, Pocahontas is remembered for the important part she played in the growth of the Jamestown colony. She will always be a part of history.

GLOSSARY

captured (KAP-churd) Took control of by force.

colonists (KAH-luh-nists) People who live in a colony.

colony (KAH-luh-nee) A new place where people move that is still ruled by the leaders of the country from which they came.

custom (KUS-tum) A practice common to a person or people in a place.

explored (ek-SPLORD) Traveled over little-known land.

explosion (ek-SPLOH-zhun) When something blows up.

historians (hih-STOR-ee-unz) People who study the past.

kidnapped (KID-napt) Carried off by force.

lifestyle (LYF-styl) The manner in which a person lives.

ritual (RIH-choo-ul) Special actions done for reasons of faith.

starvation (star-VAY-shun) The act of suffering or dying from hunger.

tribe (TRYB) A group of people who share the same customs, language, and relatives.

INDEX

WEB SITES

Due to the changing nature of Internet links, PowerKids Press has developed an online list of Web sites related to the subject of this book. This site is updated regularly. Please use this link to access the list:
www.powerkidslinks.com/wrh/pocahont/